F205.4 .W3 W56

23434

ADDRESS

OF THE

WASHINGTON

NATIONAL MONUMENT SOCIETY

TO THE

PEOPLE OF THE UNITED STATES,

WITH AN

APPENDIX,

Containing Proceedings of the Society at the Inauguration Meeting of 22d March, 1859; Report of the Select Committee of the House of Representatives appointed to consider the Memorial of the Society, made on the 22d February, 1855; and the Charter of the Society.

WASHINGTON:
GEO. S. GIDEON, PRINTER.
1859.

WASHINGTON NATIONAL MONUMENT.

To the People of the United States.

Commended to you by a charter from Congress, the WASHINGTON NATIONAL MONUMENT SOCIETY invites your prompt, earnest, and persevering action in completing the Monument to the FATHER OF HIS COUNTRY at the National Metropolis.

The universal custom of nations, civilized and barbarous, to commemorate by monumental representations remarkable events in their history, and their gratitude to great public benefactors, is evidence that such testimonials are prompted by a feeling natural to the human heart. Experience has shown that in free States their tendency is to cherish public spirit, devotion to liberty, and generous emulation of the patriotism which incited to deeds thus honored by the community. The life of GEORGE WASHINGTON is the history of the American Revolution and of the foundation of the American Republic; events equaling in dignity and importance any other, and, in their influence on human freedom and progress, surpassing all others, in the annals of our race. His personal character is hailed by the consenting voice of the whole world as a model of excellence—solitary, transcendent, unapproached. Men of all descriptions, and everywhere, take pride in his name. It is the watchword of liberty in every land; it is heard with mingled respect and apprehension in the palaces of kings; with reverence in the hut of the savage. Men of the most discordant principles; men who have agreed in nothing else; friends of liberty like Fox and Erskine and Brougham; despots like Napoleon; have united in according to Washington the loftiest place in the temple of human glory, and in considering his example as a precious legacy to all mankind. Since his death, almost sixty years have passed, and yet the nation which, under Providence, was created by his valor, his wisdom, and his virtue, has (unless the erection of his statue in 1841, on the Capitol grounds, can be so regarded,) hitherto reared no monument to his memory. Of this strange neglect an explanation not less strange is sometimes given It has been said that his countrymen deeply feel and cordially acknowledge his pre-eminence, and the vast, incalculable debt of gratitude which they owe to him; that he is enshrined in their affections and veneration; that material monuments, however suitable to other illustrious men, are inappropriate to him; and that his true monument already exists in the heart of every American. This doctrine, as perverse in logic as in morals, is the casuistry of an indolent patriotism, which, almost confessing that a high public duty has been neglected, seeks shelter and excuse in a cloud of declamation. From such reasoning the glowing hearts of the American people resile. They feel, if Washington did indeed render services to his country more exalted in their nature, more comprehensive in their scope, and more enduring in their consequences, than individual man had ever before rendered to social man, then that his country, instead of refusing a monument to his memory, owes it to her own character and to the cause of human liberty, to build one which shall be nobler than any former monument ever erected in honor of a mortal. This is the logic of American common sense and American right feeling.

The art of sculpture has often been employed to commemorate the deeds of WASHINGTON and his country's gratitude. Virginia, his native State; her noble neighbors, on one side Maryland, on the other North Carolina; other States, cities, and rural districts, throughout the Union, have, at different times, honored by monumental memorials his services and his principles of action—principles which are the very salt of a Republic. On the 22d of June, 1784, the Legislature of Virginia passed a resolution for procuring a statue of WASHINGTON of the "finest marble and best workmanship," with the following inscription on its pedestal, viz: "The General Assembly of the Commonwealth of Virginia have caused this statue to be erected as a monument of affection and gratitude to GEORGE WASHINGTON, who, uniting to the endowments of the hero the virtues of the patriot, and exerting both in establishing the liberties of his country, has rendered his name dear to his fellow-citizens and given the world an immortal example of true glory. Done in the year," &c.

The foregoing resolution was promptly carried into effect. The statue ordered by it was executed by Houdon, and now stands in the capitol at Richmond. At the same place, on the 22d of February, 1858, was inaugurated, with imposing ceremonies and in the presence of an enthusiastic multitude, an equestrian statue of WASHINGTON, which had been ordered by the Legislature and executed by Crawford, a native artist, whose genius was the pride of his country, and whose early death she mourns.

In the same year, (1784,) in which the State of Virginia ordered a statue of WASHINGTON to be erected, she offered to him a magnificent gift in connexion with the great scheme, originating with himself, of intercommunication of the Atlantic and Western waters. "It is the desire," said the Legislature, "of the representatives of this Commonwealth to embrace every suitable occasion of testifying their sense of the *unexampled merits* of GEORGE WASHINGTON, ESQ., towards his country, and it is their wish in particular that those great works for its improvement, which, both as springing from the liberty which he has been so instrumental in establishing, and as encouraged by his patronage, will be durable monuments of his glory, may be made monuments also of the gratitude of his country." The extraordinary circumstances of this benefaction made its offer embarrassing to WASHINGTON. But, obeying a rule which he had early prescribed to himself, and never swerved from, he declined the offer, as a personal gift, but consented to receive it in trust for public objects. Some time before his death he assigned a portion of it—one hundred shares in the James River Company—to the now flourishing seminary of learning in Rockbridge county, Virginia, known as "Washington College." The other portion—fifty shares in the Potomac Company—he bequeathed for the endowment of a college in the District of Columbia. These shares are supposed to be held in trust by the Chesapeake and Ohio Canal Company, as successors of the Potomac Company.

After peace had been proclaimed, the continental Congress, on the 7th of August, 1783, resolved unanimously, "That an equestrian statue of General Washington be erected at the place where the residence of Congress shall be established;" and directed that the statue should be supported by a marble pedestal, on which should be represented four principal events of the Revolutionary war, in which he commanded in person. On the pedestal were to be engraved the following words:

"The United States, in Congress assembled, ordered this statue to be erected, in the year of our Lord 1783, in honor of George Washington, the illustrious Commander-in-Chief of the Armies of the United States of America, during the war which vindicated and secured their liberty, sovereignty, and independence."

When Congress in 1783, and Virginia in 1784, ordained monumental memorials in honor of Washington, the closing act in the great drama of his life had not been performed. His character, though then illustrious beyond rivalry, was still incomplete. He was the hero, the patriot, the triumphant champion of human rights and public liberty, the founder of an Empire. But events were yet to come, bringing with them the crowning glory of his character. In the exercise of the great and extraordinary powers conferred upon him as the leader of our armies, he had indeed shown, in his camp, that he possessed civic abilities of the highest order. But they were not brought into full display till he became the Chief of the new Federal Government. It was then that he earned his last, perhaps proudest, title to the gratitude of his country, and the veneration of the world, as a wise ruler.

On the death of WASHINGTON a joint committee of the two Houses of Congress was appointed to consider on the most suitable manner of paying honor to his memory. Among the resolutions adopted on their report was one, "That a marble monument be erected by the United States, at the city of Washington, and that the family of GENERAL WASHINGTON be requested to permit his body to be deposited under it; and that the monument be so designed as to commemorate the great events of his military and political life." A copy of the resolutions was transmitted to his widow by the President of the United States. "Taught,"— she says in her most touching and impressive answer, "taught by the great example which I have *so long had before me, never to oppose my private wishes to the public will*, I must consent to the request made by Congress, which you have had the goodness to transmit to me; and in doing this I *need not, I cannot say, what a sacrifice of individual feeling I make* to a sense of public duty." Alas! the sacrifice was useless as it was painful. The resolution of Congress which asked for it is to this day a dead letter. [See note at page 17.]

On the 8th of May, 1800, the committee made a further report to the House of Representatives, on which the House passed a resolution "that a mausoleum be erected for GEORGE WASHINGTON in the city of Washington."

On the 1st of January, 1801, the House of Representatives passed a bill appropriating $200,000 for the erection of the mausoleum.

On the 15th of January, 1824, Mr. BUCHANAN, now President of the United States, than a member of the House of Representatives, offered to that body the following resolution:

"*Resolved*, That a committee be appointed, whose duty it shall be to inquire in what manner the resolutions of Congress, passed on the 24th of December, 1799, relative to the erection of a marble monument in the Capitol, at the city of Washington, to commemorate the great events of the military and political life of GENERAL WASHINGTON, may be best accomplished, and that they have leave to report by bill or otherwise."

The resolution was, after discussion, laid on the table.

This is believed to be the last proceeding in Congress on the subject until a recent period. [See note at page 17.]

The resolutions of Congress which have been referred to, having remained unexecuted as late as 1833, some citizens of Washington, whose names were a passport to public confidence, formed in that year a voluntary association for erecting *"a great national monument to the memory of Washington, at the seat of the Federal Government."* They invoked the people to redeem the plighted faith of the Representatives of the people and the States. Among the founders of the society the name of George Watterston, now deceased, calls for special notice on this occasion. With him originated the conception of the enterprise. He was the Secretary of the Society from its beginning to his death, in February, 1854; conducted its extensive correspondence, prepared its numerous publications; and, in every branch of its business, devoted his time and energies to its object, with a zeal as effective as it was ardent, constant, and disinterested.

The Washington National Monument Society commenced its pious work under the highest, the most animating auspices. John Marshall, the great Chief Justice, was its first President. On his death, in 1835, he was succeeded by ex-President Madison. The language of the "Father of the Constitution" in accepting the appointment is, like all else from his pen, memorable. He was then in the 85th year of his age. "I am very sensible," said he, "of the distinction conferred by the relations in which the society has placed me; and feeling, like my illustrious predecessor, a deep interest in the object of the association, I cannot withhold, as an evidence of it, the acceptance of the appointment; though aware that in my actual condition it cannot be more than honorary, and that under no circumstances could it supply the loss which the society has sustained.

"A monument worthy the memory of Washington, reared by the means proposed, will commemorate at the same time a virtue, a patriotism, and a gratitude truly national, with which the friends of liberty everywhere will sympathize, and of which our country may always be proud."

The first Vice President of the Society was Judge WILLIAM CRANCH, eminent as a learned jurist, as a just and impartial magistrate, and for the purity of his life.

The progress of the Society was at first slow. In order that all might have an opportunity to contribute, the amount to be received from any one person was limited to $1 a year. This restriction was removed in 1845. In 1836 about $28,000 had been collected. This fund was placed in the hands of General NATHAN TOWSON, SAMUEL HARRISON SMITH, and THOMAS MUNROE, gentlemen of the highest respectability. Under their faithful and judicious management it was invested, as was also the interest accruing on it, in good stocks. The financial difficulties of the country, beginning in 1837, suspended collections for several years. In 1847, the aggregate of collections and accumulated interest was $87,000, which amount was deemed sufficient to justify the Society in beginning the erection of the monument. On the 31st of January, 1848, Congress passed a resolution authorizing the Washington National Monument Society to erect "a monument to the memory of GEORGE WASHINGTON upon such portion of the public grounds or reservations within the city of Washington, not otherwise occupied, as shall be selected by the President of the United States and the Board of Managers of said Society, as a suitable site on which to erect the said monument, and for the necessary protection thereof." The site selected, under the authority of this resolution, was the public reservation numbered 3 on the plan of the city of Washington, containing upwards of thirty acres, near the Potomac river, directly west of the Capitol, and south of the President's House. The grant was executed, on the 12th of April, 1849, by the President of the United States and the Board of Managers of the Society, and is duly recorded among the land records of the District of Columbia. The site selected presents a beautiful view of the Potomac; is so elevated that the monument will be seen from all parts of the city and the surrounding country, and, being a public reservation, it is safe from any future obstruction of the view. It is so near the river that materials for constructing the monument can be conveyed to it from the river at but

little expense; stone, sand, and lime, all of the best kind, can be brought to it by water from convenient distances; and marble of the most beautiful quality, obtained at a distance of only eleven miles from Baltimore, on the Susquehanna railroad, can be brought either on the railroad or in vessels. In addition to these and kindred reasons, the adoption of the site was farther and impressively recommended by the consideration, that the monument to be erected on it would be in full view of Mount Vernon, where rest the ashes of the Chief; and by evidence that WASHINGTON himself, whose unerring judgment had selected this city to be the capital of the nation, had also selected this particular spot for "a monument to the American Revolution," which in the year 1795 it was proposed should "be erected or placed at the permanent seat of government of the United States." This monument was to have been executed by Ceracchi, a Roman sculptor, and paid for by contributions of individuals. The same site is marked on Major L'Enfant's map of Washington city for the equestrian statue of GENERAL WASHINGTON, ordered by Congress in 1783; which map was examined, approved, and transmitted to Congress by him when President of the United States.

A plan for the monument was adopted, after wide consultation with experienced and judicious experts, and a careful comparison of the various plans submitted, as well with each other as with an ideal standard of excellence. The one selected proposed an obelisk 517 feet high, and a pantheon or base. The obelisk was estimated to cost $552,000, and the whole work, including obelisk and pantheon, $1,122,000.

The anniversary of American Independence was chosen as a fit day for laying the corner-stone of a monument to its hero. On the 4th of July, 1848, under a bright sky, in the presence of the President and Vice President of the United States, Senators and Representatives in Congress, the Heads of the Executive Departments, and other officers, Executive and Judicial, of the Government, the Corporate Authorities of Washington, Georgetown, and Alexandria, military companies, associations of many descriptions, delegations from States and Territories of the Union

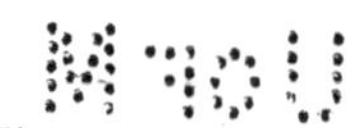

and from several Indian tribes, and a countless multitude, ROBERT C. WINTHROP, Speaker of the House of Representatives, pronounced an eloquent oration on the occasion; other addresses were delivered; and the corner-stone was laid of a "Great National Monument to the memory of Washington at the seat of the Federal Government." The board of managers at once commenced active operations, which were vigorously prosecuted. In about six years from the laying of the corner-stone they were enabled to raise the obelisk to the height of 170 feet, being a little more than one-third of its proposed ultimate elevation. On the work as thus far done $230,000, the whole amount of collections, including interest on investments, from the origin of the society, were expended. The foundation of the obelisk was laid eighty-one feet square, eight feet below the surface of the ground, and the obelisk is contracted in its progress so as to be sixty-one feet ten inches at the top, an elevation of twenty-five feet of solid masonry. It is commenced at the height of seventeen and a half feet above the ground, fifty-five feet square, cased with marble, with walls fifteen feet thick, leaving a cavity of twenty-five feet. It will be ascended by stairs in the inside, and by machinery. The purchase of materials and the general construction of the work were committed by the Board of Managers to three of their number, denominated a Building Committee, subject to the revisory authority of the Board, which met weekly. The services of the Board were gratuitous. Faithful to the principles on which the Society had acted from the beginning, they solicited contributions from the whole people, without distinction of party, or sect, or creed; and in the same national spirit administered, in all respects, the trust confided to them.

In 1854 the Board of Managers presented a memorial to Congress, giving a brief history of the Monument enterprise, and stating that all recent efforts on their part to obtain means for completing the work had proved abortive; that they were unable to devise any plan more likely to succeed; and that under these circumstances they brought the subject before Congress for such action as Congress might deem proper. The memorial was referred in the House of Representatives to a select committee of thirteen members, of which committee HENRY MAY, of Maryland, was chairman. On the 22d of February, 1855, MR. MAY, from the select committee, made a most able and eloquent report, in which, after a careful examination of the whole subject, the proceedings of the Society were reviewed and strongly approved, and a subscription recommended of $200,000 by Congress "on behalf of the people of the United States, to aid the funds of the Society." This, it will be recollected, is the sum which the House of Representatives, by their resolution of January 1st, 1801, had agreed to appropriate for a mausoleum to WASHINGTON in the city of Washington.

The report of the select committee was made under favoring circumstances. But on the very day of its presentment the Managers of the Society were unexpectedly superseded in their places by an unlawful election. We purposely forbear on this occasion any comment on that proceeding and its consequences, except the remark that the experiment of constructing the Monument through the agency of a *party* signally failed. After this experiment had been abandoned by its projectors the enterprise passed into the hands of gentlemen who, after making suitable arrangements for the conservation of the Monument and protection of the grounds and other property connected with it, on the 20th of October last surrendered them to the Board which was ejected from office by the transaction of February 22d, 1855. Admonished by that transaction and its results of the legal difficulties in the way of a voluntary association, consisting of members residing in all parts of the Union, we had applied to Congress for a charter. This was at length granted. On the 22d of February, 1859, an act passed Congress, and was approved by the President on the 26th, incorporating "The Washington National Monument Society." By one of its provisions the President of the United States for the time being is *ex officio* President of the Society, and the Governors of the several States of the United States are respectively *ex officio* its Vice Presidents.

On resuming the administration of the Monument affairs, we found that during the interruption there had been added to its obelisk, which we had left at the height of 170 feet, only two courses of marble, each two feet high; that of this a sufficient quantity of marble was on the ground on the 22d of February, 1855, dressed and finished, and ready for setting, to make a course, and of the other a number of rough blocks of marble were on hand; and that it was dressed by the persons in possession, and the residue made up of condemned marble which had been accumulating for years. We found also numerous repairs to be necessary, which the building committee were instructed to make, so far as the means of the Society would allow, in order to preserve the property, and in view of as early a resumption of the work as might be possible.

In accordance with our former system, it is our purpose to solicit contributions from the people of the United States, through the instrumentality of agents, of known or well attested integrity and intelligence, who will be required to give adequate security for the faithful discharge of their duties; to invoke aid, at suitable times, from Congress, from State and Territorial Legislatures, and from the voluntary associations, formed for diversified and meritorious objects, which overspread our country. The intended appeal to the States has by one of them been generously anticipated. The Legislature of the young State of California recently passed an act appropriating *one thousand dollars annually* in aid of the monument.

Seventy-five years ago, in the course of an extensive Western journey, the eagle eye of Washington descried the political necessity and the practicability of opening a communication between the head-waters of the Potomac and the tributaries of the Ohio river. In a private letter on that subject to a friend, written in the following year, after deprecating commercial connexions between the Western States and foreign Governments, he speaks of "the country of California" as "being still more to the westward, and belonging to another Power." California! Now one of the sovereign States of the American Union, and the first of them all to pay the debt of gratitude to its founder by aiding in the erection of a monument to him at the seat of the Federal Government. Brighter, more glorious, is this act than are all her golden treasures. May her sister States soon imitate her example!

"Each State," said the Select Committee of the House of Representatives in their report in 1855, "and two of the Territories of the Union, have contributed a block of marble or stone, inscribed with its arms or some suitable inscription or device, and a great many others have been offered by various institutions and societies throughout the land; and several foreign Governments have testified their desire to unite in this great work of humanity, intended to commemorate the virtues of its chief ornament and example. The boundaries of Christendom do not limit his fame, which reaches to the remotest parts of the earth, and the most distant and isolated nations have testified their veneration towards his memory. Switzerland, Rome, Bremen, Turkey, Greece, China, and Japan, have piously united to pay their homage to our Washington. Such tributes are our *highest trophies*. The history of mankind affords no parallel to this."

To the testimonials described by the committee others of a similar character have been recently added, and more will doubtless be offered.

Having in the past been honored by your confidence, we hope to receive it in the future. We shall strive to deserve it by maintaining the principles and the policy on the ground of which it was acquired. We return to our labors expecting you justly to estimate and candidly to allow for the circumstances under which they are resumed. We find an empty treasury: an enterprise now in a state of suspended animation is to be resuscitated: the arrangements and connexions through which it had been formerly prosecuted are dissolved: new instrumentalities are to be provided: an interval of inaction or pernicious activity has continued for four years: and into the minds of some of you distrust may have been infused. But such considerations do not discourage us. We appeal to the great heart of the American People; we invoke them to come forward promptly, one and all, and rescue their good name from the opprobrium of ingratitude to WASHINGTON: to him whom, in the first agony of a nation's bereavement, her Representatives, with tearful eyes and bleeding hearts, proclaimed—whom an admiring world confessed—and whom history has decreed to be—"FIRST IN WAR, FIRST IN PEACE, AND FIRST IN THE HEARTS OF HIS COUNTRYMEN." In the success of this appeal our confidence is unfaltering. The character of the people of the United States furnishes abundant grounds for the confidence. A single, and of itself a sufficient one, is that our object will find untiring and persuasive advocates among the women of the United States. Indignant at a sixty years' apathy in the other sex, they came forward, but yesterday as it were, with an almost simultaneous impulse in all sections of the Union, and said that one stipulation at least of the public faith, in relation to the Father of his Country, should no longer go unperformed. They said that so much of the resolution of Congress in 1799 as pledged the national faith to guard from desecration and the contingencies of fortune the mortal remains of WASHINGTON, should at once, without another moment of delay, be carried out. What they said, they did. They will soon be the guardians of the grave of WASHINGTON.

If the spirits of the "just made perfect" are permitted to look down on earth and to sympathize with mortals, we can imagine no tribute more grateful to the spirit of WASHINGTON than the spectacle of his countrywomen as the self-elected, perpetual watchers at his tomb. Of all the numerous testimonies of public veneration and affection which were offered to him in 1789, on his journey from Mount Vernon to New York, to be there inaugurated as the first President of the United States, none is said to have so touched his heart as an incident connected with his reception at Trenton. "The gentler sex," says the historian, "prepared in their own taste a tribute of applause, indicative of the grateful recollection in which they held their deliverance, twelve years before, from an insulting enemy. On the bridge over the creek which passes through the town was erected a triumphal arch, highly ornamented with laurel and flowers, and supported by thirteen pillars, each entwined with wreaths of evergreen. On the front of the arch was inscribed in large gilt letters, '*The Defender of the Mothers will be the Protector of the Daughters.*' * * * At this place he was met by a party of matrons, leading their daughters dressed in white, who carried baskets of flowers in their hands, and sang with exquisite sweetness an ode of two stanzas, composed for the occasion." The flowers referred to in its last line were then strewed before him.

Guardians of the grave of WASHINGTON! A holy office; holier than that of the pious Vestals who guarded the sacred fire of Rome: An office sought and won in the spirit which animated American women in the trying scenes of the Revolution: An office well suited to the social position, at once lofty and unobtrusive, of American women in the American Republic. Twenty years ago the peculiarities of this position were perceived by a foreign observer of our country and its institutions, whom an enlightened public opinion has justly placed by the side of Montesquieu. After explaining these peculiarities, De Tocqueville adds:

"If I were asked, now that I am drawing to the close of this work, in which I have spoken of so many important things done by the Americans, to what the singular prosperity and growing strength of that people ought to be attributed, I should reply, to the superiority of their women."

The French philosopher has lived to witness another and a crowning illustration of his eulogy. He has seen the duty of patriotism to the ashes of WASHINGTON, so long neglected by husbands, and fathers, and brothers, assumed and discharged by the matrons and the maidens of our land. Heaven has blessed their efforts. May their energies be now directed to another and kindred duty of their country to the memory of WASHINGTON! May their persuasive example, their just influence, and their active sympathies waken husbands, and fathers, and brothers to the duty of erecting a monument to WASHINGTON worthy of his name and of the American People!

By order of the Society:

JOHN CARROLL BRENT, *Sec'y.*

WASHINGTON NATIONAL MONUMENT OFFICE, *May* 17, 1859.

Note to Pages 7 and 8.

On the 13th of February, 1832, a report was made to the Senate of the United States by Mr. Clay, and to the House of Representatives by Mr. Philemon Thomas, chairmen, respectively, of committees to make arrangements for celebrating the approaching centennial anniversary of Washington's birthday. One of the resolutions authorized the President of the Senate and the Speaker of the House of Representatives "to make application to John A. Washington, of Mount Vernon, for the body of George Washington, to be removed and deposited in the Capitol at Washington city, in conformity with the resolution of Congress of the 24th December, 1799; and that if they obtain the requisite consent to the removal thereof, they be further authorized to cause it to be removed and deposited in the Capitol on the 22d day of February, 1832." This resolution does not suggest any connexion between the removal of the remains and their being deposited under a monument, as proposed by the resolution of 1799. It is understood that when the report of the joint committee was made, one of the standing committees of the House of Representatives had under consideration the erecting of a marble statue of Washington, to be executed by Mr. Greenough, and, as was then expected, to be placed in the centre of the rotundo of the Capitol. In the course of the discussion occasioned by the report, one of the speakers stated that two years before, a resolution had been submitted to the House of Representatives for the erection of a pedestrian statue of Washington in the Capitol. From a remark of Mr. Clay, the purpose seems to have been to place the remains in a vault under the centre of the rotundo.

The two Senators and several of the Representatives from Virginia opposed the removal of Washington's remains from their resting-place in his native State. Senator Tazewell referred to an application which she had made in 1816 to Judge Wasihngton, then the proprietor of Mount Vernon, for his consent to the removal of the remains to Richmond, to be deposited under a suitable monument in that city. Mr. T. represented Judge Washington to have answered: "It was impossible for him to consent to the removal, unless the remains of one of those dear relations accompanied the body." "Are the remains," asked Mr. Tazewell, "of the husband, to be removed from the side of the wife? In their lives they lived happily together, and I never will consent to divide them in death." This consideration made so strong an impression on Congress that the resolution was modified so as to ask the consent of Mr. John A. Washington, and that of Mr. George W. P. Custis, the grandson of Mrs. Martha Washington, for the removal and depositing in the Capitol at Washington city of her remains, at the same time with those of her late consort, George Washington. Mr. John A. Washington felt constrained to withhold his consent, by the fact that General Washington's will, in respect to the disposition of his remains, had been recently carried into full effect. Mr. Custis, taking a different view of that clause in the will, gave his "most hearty consent to the removal of the remains after the manner proposed," and congratulated "the Government upon the approaching consummation of a great act of national gratitude."

In the debate in the House of Representatives on the report of the joint committee, Mr. DODDRIDGE, of Virginia, remarked that he was a member of the legislature of that State when the transaction of 1816 took place, and "he felt entirely satisfied that the resolution for removing the remains to Richmond would never have passed the Assembly of Virginia but for the loss of all hope that Congress would act in the matter."

Mr. McDUFFIE opposed the removal of the remains from Mount Vernon. But, said he, "As to a monument, rear it; spend upon it what you will; make it durable as the pyramids, eternal as the mountains; you shall have my co-operation. Erect, if you please, a mausoleum to the memory of WASHINGTON in the Capitol, and let it be as splendid as art can make it."

The refusal of the proprietor of Mount Vernon to permit the removal of the remains was regarded by Mr. CLAY as a new reason why the pending resolution for erecting a statue of WASHINGTON at the Capitol should prevail. "An image,"—he said, "a testimonial of this great man, the Father of his Country, should exist in every part of the Union, as a memorial of his patriotism and of the services rendered his country; but of all places it was required in this Capital, the centre of the Union, the offspring, the creation of his mind and of his labors."

The pedestrian statue of WASHINGTON by Greenough, ordered in 1832, was placed in the rotundo in 1841, and afterwards removed to the east park. In 1853 Congress appropriated $50,000 for the erection, by Clark Mills, of an equestrian statue of WASHINGTON.

APPENDIX.

ORGANIZATION OF THE SOCIETY UNDER THE CHARTER.

The meeting for the organization of the Washington National Monument Society, under the act of incorporation granted by Congress at its recent session, took place on Tuesday evening, 22d March, 1859, in the Aldermen's Chamber, in the City Hall.

The chair was taken at a few minutes past 7 o'clock by the PRESIDENT OF THE UNITED STATES, as *ex officio* President of the Society.

Mr. FENDALL then rose and said :

Mr. President : The illness and consequent absence of a distinguished member of this Society devolves on me the unexpected duty of welcoming you to this chamber. Here, more than a quarter of a century ago, a few patriotic citizens assembled and founded the Washington National Monument Society. Of those individuals only four, it is believed, now survive. On the death of WASHINGTON, Congress passed a resolution to erect a monument to the memory of that greatest and best of men ; but years rolled on and this sacred duty remained undischarged. The object of this Society was to waken the hearts of the people to fulfil the neglected promise of their representatives, and to redeem the republic from the reproach of ingratitude to its founder. The earnest efforts of an association of private individuals to effect this purpose have been sustained by their fellow-citizens and approved by Congress. The monument has been elevated to about one-third of its proposed height. A committee of the House of Representatives, after a careful examination of the proceedings of the Society, reported an emphatic approval of its conduct, and recommended a liberal subscription on the part of Congress towards completing the monument ; and, more recently, Congress has given the Society the power of self-protection by granting to it a charter of incorporation. It has now here assembled for organization under this charter ; and on an occasion so interesting to its future prospects it was deemed proper to request the presence of the President of the United States as *ex officio* President of this Society. Oppressed as the Chief Magistrate of this great nation must be with the cares of state, his compliance with this request is felt by the Society to be a gracious act, which cannot fail to exert an auspicious influence on their labors.

They look forward to the effect of this high example in stimulating their fellow-citizens to unite in the vigorous prosecution of a work dear to patriotism and to national honor. Undoubtedly the proudest of all monuments is that already raised to the fame of WASHINGTON in the hearts of his countrymen, in the applause of all mankind, and in a memory which will descend to the last posterity. But all history shows that the erection of national monuments in honor of great national benefactors is a form of public gratitude so universal as to be closely allied to the sentiment itself; and that, when a nation forgets the glory of its great men, it ceases to be worthy of them. The completion of the monument now in progress is far more important to the fame of the American people than to the fame of WASHINGTON.

In the name, and on behalf of the Society, I take leave, sir, to thank you for your presence and co-operation on this occasion.

The PRESIDENT said, that before proceeding to the business of organization, he would make a few remarks in reference to his connexion with this matter, when, thirty-four or thirty-five years ago, he was a member of the House of Representatives. At that time, a young man and a new member, he offered a resolution the object of which was to redeem the plighted faith of the country to erect a monument to him to whom its warmest gratitude was due. He did not remember at whose instance he did this, but it was undoubtedly at the instance of some respectable citizens of Washington, who remembered the obligations which had been incurred by the previous action of the national legislature. All must recollect that after the death of WASHINGTON Congress passed a resolution to erect a monument to his memory, and a respectful communication was addressed to Mrs. Washington requesting the body of the deceased to be placed within it. What was the reply he (the President) did not now recollect; but so the matter remained till 1823 or 1824, when he himself brought it before Congress. He was a young man then, and perhaps there was something of the sophomore in his dealings with the subject, but he pressed it with all the ardor of youth. No doubt if any one were to examine the files of the National Intelligencer of the year 1823 or 1824, his speech would be found there reported. It was considered at that time, and was so remarked in Congress, that it was rather an indignity that any effort should be made to raise a monument to the honor and memory of WASHINGTON besides that which existed in the hearts of his countrymen. The President did not remember what was done, but he did remember the extreme mortification which he suffered from the ill success of his movement. To attempt to pronounce any eulogy on WASHINGTON would be vain. Not only in this country is his name loved and revered beyond that of all other men, but abroad, where he had been a good deal, in foreign lands our country is illustrated by him, and his name is never mentioned but as that of the purest, most unselfish patriot that ever lived; not only the most unselfish, but the most self-sacrificing of whom history kept record. It is vain to say that no painting or no sculpture of such men should be preserved. It is a duty the people owe to themselves to see that this work shall go on; and whilst he would not say it is a reproach, it is a reflection on the people of this country that the resolution of Congress made sixty years ago should have been peimitted to lie a dead letter upon the statute-book. The President thought in his remarks made in the House of Representatives in 1824 or 1825 some of the objects and advantages sought to be secured by the present Society were alluded to. He would now proceed to organize the Society.

On motion of Mr. LENOX, Mr. J. C. BRENT was chosen Secretary of the meeting.

On motion of Capt. CARBERY, the following resolutions were unanimously adopted:

1. *Resolved*, That the charter granted to this Society by the act of Congress passed on the 22d and approved on the 26th of February, in the year 1859, and entitled "An act to incorporate the Washington National Monument Society," be accepted, and that said charter be the constitution of this Society.

2. That this Society shall hold an annual meeting on the 22d day of February in every year, and such other meetings as may hereafter be prescribed or called.

3. That the officers of this Society, in addition to those prescribed by the charter, shall be a First Vice President, who shall be the Mayor of Washington for the time being *ex officio*, and a Second and Third Vice Presidents, a Treasurer, and a Secretary, to be now elected, and to continue in office till the annual meeting on the 22d day of February next.

4. That the Second and Third Vice Presidents, the Treasurer, and the Secretary shall be elected at the annual meeting on the 22d of February of every year: *Provided*, That all officers shall continue in office till their successors are respectively duly appointed.

5. That a committee of three members be appointed to prepare and report at a meeting of the society to be held on Tuesday, the 12th of April next, a plan for carrying out its objects, and by-laws and regulations for the conduct of business, and defining and prescribing the duties of officers and agents.

6. That a committee of three members be appointed to prepare and report at the meeting named in the fifth resolution an Address to the People of the United States.

7. That the Secretary shall forward a copy of the charter to each corporator, and request him to state whether or not he accepts the trust, and will be able punctually to attend the meetings of the society.

On motion of Mr. WM. A. BRADLEY, the blanks in the resolutions appointing committees were filled each with the number three; when, it having been agreed that the committees should be appointed by the President, the following gentlemen were appointed, viz: on the committee to prepare a constitution, by-laws, &c., Col. Force, Mr. J. B. H. Smith, and Mr. John C. Brent; on the committee to address the public, Mr. Fendall, Gen. Walter Jones, and Mr. Walter Lenox.

Mr. J. B. H. SMITH moved that the society proceed to elect officers for the purpose of organizing the corporation; when, it having been resolved to elect by ballot, the following officers were elected:

General WINFIELD SCOTT, 2d Vice President.

THOMAS CARBERY, 3d Vice President.

J. B. H. SMITH, Treasurer.

JOHN C. BRENT, Secretary.

Mr. RICHARD S. COXE said that for some reason or other he had never become connected with this society. He had, however, always sympathized with it, and he acknowledged the warmest wishes for its furtherance and success. He was aware that difficulties and disputes had arisen in the course of its history, but with them he had never had any connexion. The only objection he had ever heard to the society was just the one the President had alluded to in his remarks, namely, that the only proper monument for WASHINGTON is a monument in the hearts of his countrymen. This objection he deemed one of the most puerile and ridiculous he had ever heard uttered.

Is it because a man stands high in the world's respect, because he is embalmed in its memory, that he deserves no testimonial of this sort? Is it for this that no national monument is to be raised to tell men of his worth and glory? Such reasoning would imply that we are to erect monuments only to those who are undeserving. Is it not the highest ground to take that the memory of the man first in the world's respect should be perpetuated to them that did not know him and did not live in his time?

Mr. C. hoped the project now in hand would be carried out and terminate in complete success. It had been said by orators of Great Britain, to which country WASHINGTON was opposed, against which he warred, that of all the men of history the purest and most disinterested was WASHINGTON. Mr. C. earnestly wished all prosperity to the institution, and was delighted at its resuscitation, and was also delighted at hearing the narrative of the part already taken by the President in furtherance of the object for which the meeting was now assembled.

Mr. LENOX rose to move that the society now adjourn; when,

The PRESIDENT asked to say a few words in connexion with the remarks of Mr. COXE. The day had gone by when the monument of WASHINGTON should be left to rest alone in the hearts of his countrymen. This is the city called by him into existence—called by his name—and the most appropriate place in the world for a monument to his memory, to tower to the skies. The appeal to build this monument will never be made to the American people in vain. In the mountains, in the valleys, the appeal will be answered with cheerfulness, as each one of the people of the whole nation will feel the honor he does himself in contributing towards a becoming testimonial to the Father of his Country.

The society, said the President, has been organized under the happiest auspices, and he had no doubt that in less than ten years the monument would be completed. If Congress will not regard the wishes of the people in helping to raise this monument, the people will do it themselves. The cause ought not to be allowed to slumber. Let us, therefore, said the President, like faithful sentinels, make proper appeals, and my life for it such appeals will be successful.

Mr. LENOX renewed his motion to adjourn, which was passed, and the society adjourned, to meet at its next regular period.

JAMES BUCHANAN,

President of the United States, and ex officio President of the Society.

JOHN CARROLL BRENT, *Secretary.*

REPORT

OF THE

SELECT COMMITTEE.

33d Congress, 2d Session. | HOUSE OF REPRESENTATIVES. | Report No. 94.

Monument to the Memory of Washington.

[To accompany joint resolution no. 58.]—February 22, 1855.

On the 13th of July, 1854, it was resolved that a select committee of thirteen members be appointed to consider the memorial of the Washington National Monument Society, and the following gentlemen were appointed the members of the committee:

Mr. MAY, *of Maryland, Chairman.*
Mr. J. GLANCY JONES, *of Penn.*
Mr. REESE, *of Georgia.*
Mr. PURYEAR, *of North Carolina.*
Mr. HASTINGS, *of New York.*
Mr. ELIOT, *of Massachusetts.*
Mr. OLIVER, *of Missouri.*
Mr. PRATT, *of Connecticut.*
Mr. ELLISON, *of Ohio.*
Mr. VAIL, *of New Jersey.*
Mr. McMULLEN, *of Virginia.*
Mr. MACY, *of Wisconsin.*
Mr. DOWDELL, *of Alabama.*

REPORT.

Mr. May, from the Select Committee on the Washington National Monument, made the following report:

The Select Committee of Thirteen, to whom was referred the memorial of the Board of Managers of the Washington National Monument Society, beg leave to report:

That this memorial states, "that in the year 1833, an association of individuals was formed in this city for the purpose of raising funds, by appeal to the patriotism of the people, for the erection of a monument, in the national metropolis, to the memory of the Father of his Country.

"That your memorialists, and their predecessors, elected managers of the association, have gratuitously given their services, at great personal sacrifice, to the promotion of its objects; that they have been enabled to raise the proposed monument to the height of 170 feet; that 347 feet remain yet to be erected; that the funds of the association are entirely exhausted; and all recent efforts on the part of your memorialists to obtain means for completing the work have proved abortive, and that your memorialists are unable to devise any plan more likely to succeed.

"Under these circumstances, they feel it to be their duty to bring to the notice of the representatives of the States and people of the Union these facts, in order that such action may be had on them as to the assembled wisdom and patriotism of the nation may seem meet.

"ARCH. HENDERSON, *First Vice President.*
"ELISHA WHITTLESEY, *General Agent.*
"JOHN CARROLL BRENT, *Secretary.*"

It will be seen that no specific prayer is presented; but upon the facts stated above, the society submits it to the wisdom of Congress to provide such measures as may be appropriate to the subject.

Your committee conceive that the duty is devolved upon them, on the part of the House of Representatives, to recommend such measures; and being deeply impressed with all the associations attending so interesting and hallowed a subject, they have well considered it.

As early as 1783 Congress ordered that an equestrian statue of Washington should be erected, "to testify the love, admiration, and gratitude of his countrymen;" and again, when the mournful intelligence of his death was communicated, on 24th December, 1799, that a marble monument, with suitable inscriptions, should be erected in the Capitol to the memory of Washington, and that it be "so designed as to commemorate the great events of his military and political life." It is painful to observe that these resolutions have not yet been executed. Perhaps the claims of kindred, and of his native State, have prevailed against that resolution, which ordered that his remains should be entombed beneath the monument to be erected in the Capitol. We know that his honored widow consented that this should be done; yet, Mount Vernon still holds the sacred remains of him who was "first in war, first in peace, and first in the hearts of his countrymen." Your committee could not but feel that these obligations, resolved upon, as they were, by the great and good men who were witnesses of his sublime life and character, and who were also associates of his fame, yet remain upon Congress.

Aware that a marble statue has been erected within the grounds of the Capitol, and an equestrian statue ordered by the last Congress to be raised, yet your committee think that these testimonials are not adequate to fulfil the obligation so solemnly assumed.

States and cities have raised their greatful tributes, in marble, to Washington. Maryland, near forty years ago, undertook her part in this patriotic duty, and her noble monument, at Baltimore, attests the love and gratitude of her people towards a chief whose steps their fathers so faithfully followed through the trying scenes of the Revolution. And Virginia, with gratitude unsatisfied by a faithful statue, is now raising, at Richmond, a monument, proportioned to the greatness of her son. And North Carolina, too, invoked the highest living art to present, at Raleigh, the image of the Father of his Country to the admiring eyes of her patriotic children. And memorials of public and private love and gratitude towards him are to be found throughout the land, commemorating a universal veneration. But no national tribute of adequate design has yet been raised—no offering fit to denote a country's gratitude has been constructed. Yet who shall deny that the fame of Washington deserves the grandest of human monuments, or say that such tributes can be multiplied beyond the measure of his claims?

A voluntary association of patriotic citizens of Washington, as early as 1833, conceived the purpose of erecting a national monument to the memory of Washington at the Metropolis of the republic. This association was organized under the name of "The Washington National Monument Society." Chief Justice Marshall was its first president, and after him ex-President Madison. The proposed monument was intended to be raised by the voluntary contributions of the American people. The society was organized on an admirable plan, and its officers undertook the duties assigned to them by its constitution, and have, as your committee are well satisfied, faithfully performed them.

The funds were to be collected in all parts of the United States; and agents, as competent and as faithful as could be found, were appointed, after giving bond for the performance of their duties.

These agents were sent to all parts of the country, and contributions were commenced and continued by the subscription of $1 for each person. This plan was adopted in order that all might have the opportunity to contribute.

In the appointment of these agents a careful scrutiny was exercised by the society, and undoubted recommendations of both character and capacity were in every case required; and, though an opinion may prevail in some parts of the country to the contrary, your committee are satisfied that these agents generally proved to be worthy of the confidence reposed in them.

Of the large number employed, but two of them failed to account for the money collected, and legal measures, resorted to promptly by the society against their bonds, have, in one of these instances, obtained the full amount of the liability.

It may well be questioned if any society executing a plan for collecting money so extensively has met with equal success in justifying the integrity of its agents; and it is pleasing to state that not one cent of the funds received by this society has at any time been lost by investments or otherwise.

The sum of $28,000 having been raised upon this plan, it was judiciously invested in safe funds yielding interest; and then the pulpit, the press, and the ballot-box were all invoked to aid the work; and days of sacred and patriotic associations were employed to invite a general contribution.

The restriction as to the amount of subscription being removed in 1845, the whole funds amounted by accumulations of interest then to $62,450, and the work of building the monument was at length begun in the year 1848.

An appropriate site on the banks of the Potomac was selected out of the public reservation, under a grant from Congress. Its location is most eligible. Here the first light of the morning sun will salute, and the last rays of evening rest upon its lofty head. The coincidence is striking and interesting, that the monument now in progress is on the same site which is marked on Major L'Enfant's map for the equestrian statue of Washington ordered by Congress in 1783; and that the map, after General Washington had examined and approved it, was presented by him to Congress.

Near this unfinished monument is the Smithsonian Institution. Its edifice is completed, its system in practical operation, and its annual income thirty thousand dollars. So much easier has it been found to give effect to the bounty of a benevolent foreigner, than to the gratitude of a nation to its founder.

The first object to meet the view, and inspire the patriotic feelings of the visitor to the national metropolis, the Washington Monument will stand before the eyes of the resident or sojourner as a perpetual memorial of him whose whole life was so signal an example of public virtue and patriotism.

On the 4th of July, 1848, the corner stone was laid. A plan had been selected, after careful consideration of many that were proposed, and your committee highly approve of the design.

It is a noble monument, altogether worthy of the sublime character of which it is to be a grateful testimonial.

Its foundations are deeply, broadly, and securely laid, and are sufficient to support the entire superstructure.

The work, so far as it has been performed, has been faithfully done. It appears to be plain, yet beautiful; and your committee are satisfied that it will be enduring.

Each State and two of the Territories of the Union have contributed a block of marble or stone, inscribed with its arms or some suitable device, and a great many others have been offered by various institutions and societies throughout the land; and several foreign governments have testified their desire to unite in this great work of humanity, intended to commemorate the virtues of its chief ornament and example. The boundaries of Christendom do not limit his fame, which reaches to the remotest parts of the earth, and the most distant and isolated nations have testified their veneration towards his memory. Switzerland, Rome, Bremen, Turkey, Greece, China, and Japan, have piously united to pay their homage to our Washington. Such tributes are our *highest trophies*. The history of mankind affords no parallel to this.

We feel bound, in this place, especially to commend the zeal and liberality of the Masonic societies, the order of Odd Fellows, the various fire companies, and the touching contributions of the children of the schools of the country—all regularly dedicating their affectionate tributes. And the Cherokee and Chickasaw nations of Indians also deserve to be honored for their very liberal donations of money; commemorating also in this, the eloquent sentiment of the great chief, Cornplanter, delivered to Washington in 1791: "The voice of the Seneca nation speaks to you, the great Councillor, in whose heart the wise men of all the thirteen Fires have placed their wisdom."

The shaft of the monument now reaches to the height of 170 feet. It is intended to be raised to the full height of 517 feet; so that, when completed, this monument will be proportionate to the character of its subject—the loftiest in the world.

The sum of $230,000 has been already expended upon the work, and the sum of $322,000 will be needed to complete the shaft; while the cost of the whole work, including shaft and pantheon, or base, is estimated to be $1,122,000. Let the present generation at least complete the shaft, and we may then permit those who come after us to finish the whole work.

Your committee have derived this information from the competent officers of the society, its architect, and its agents, who have charge of the work, and who have attended the sittings of the committee, explained the subject, and produced before it their plans, books, accounts, and other evidences of their transactions.

The duties of this society have demanded the constant attention of its members; and it is very gratifying to the committee to state, that neither the president, vice presidents, treasurer, secretary, nor any of the managers or members, have, from its institution, received or desired any compensation whatever. Their services have been, and will continue to be, wholly gratuitous.

We unanimously approve the plan of this monument, and of the work that has been already done; and we bear cheerful testimony to the energy, integrity, economy and patriotic love which have animated and governed the transactions of this society, and especially we commend the design of building this monument by the voluntary contributions of the people of the United States.

We do not intend to disturb this happy arrangement, or to withdraw from the exclusive jurisdiction and control of so faithful a society the completion of a work so well begun and prosecuted; we trust, and doubt not, that it will go on, with continued attention on the part of the board of managers, and of the people of the whole country.

But, at the same time, your committee think that a subscription to aid the work is due by Congress. By the faith of obligations which we have before recited, by the fact that his commission as Commander-in-Chief was bestowed on Washington by Congress, and all his glorious military services performed under their orders and authority, and by the further consideration that a sum subscribed by Congress will probably be the only mode by which each and all of the people of the United States can be said to add their share to this grateful memorial, your committee recommend that the sum of two hundred thousand dollars should be subscribed by Congress on behalf of the people of the United States, to aid the funds of the society. This was the sum devoted to the monument ordered by the resolutions of 1799, and voted by the House of Representatives on the 1st of January, 1801.

In making this recommendation we expressly disclaim engaging for any further aid by Congress to the work, on the distinct ground, that whilst it is proper Congress should make a liberal subscription towards it, yet it is both the right and duty of the people of the United States to complete it.

We canot doubt that their disposition will prove more than adequate to this result, and that this holy work should hereafter be exclusively committed to them—to the several States, cities, towns, and other organized communities of the whole country.

Assuring them, as we again do, of its noble proportions and beauty—of its solid and enduring plan and materials—of the fidelity of the work done—of the integrity, economy, energy, and system, that have marked the duties of the members of this society, and of their disinterested and patriotic zeal, we commend to the care of our countrymen this tribute of a republic's love, admiration, and gratitude towards him who, under the providence of God, was the chief author of its freedom, its dignity, and its happiness.

We report herewith a joint resolution, and subjoin the names of the officers and Board of Managers of the Society.

THE CHARTER.

AN ACT to incorporate the Washington National Monument Society.

Be it enacted by the Senate and House of Representatives of the United States of America in Congress assembled, That for the purpose of completing the erection now in progress of "a great national monument to the memory of Washington at the seat of the Federal Government," Winfield Scott, Walter Jones, John J. Abert, James Kearney, Thomas Carbery, Peter Force, William A. Bradley, Philip R. Fendall, Walter Lenox, Matthew F. Maury, and Thomas Blagden, (being the survivors of the persons mentioned in a certain grant bearing date on the twelfth day of April, in the year one thousand eight hundred and forty-eight, by James K. Polk, then President of the said United States, in virtue of a joint resolution of Congress, approved on the thirty-first day of January, in the same year, of an authority to erect a monument to the memory of George Washington, on reservation numbered three, in the said city of Washington,) and also Jonathan B. H. Smith, William W. Seaton, Elisha Whittlesey, Benjamin Ogle Tayloe, Thomas H. Crawford, William W. Corcoran, and John Carroll Brent, and their successors, to be elected in the manner hereinafter directed, shall be, and are hereby, created a corporation and body politic, by the name and style of "The Washington National Monument Society."

Sec. 2. *And be it further enacted,* That all the easements, and all and singular the rights and privileges, conveyed in the aforesaid grant, shall be, and the same hereby are, vested in and confirmed to the corporation and body politic hereinbefore created; and that any and all property and right of property of any and every kind and description whatsoever, whether in possession, or in action, or in expectancy, which may at any time before the passing of this act have been acquired by the voluntary association heretofore known by the name of the Washington National Monument Society, or which may hereafter be acquired by the corporation and body politic hereinbefore created, shall be and the same hereby are vested in and confirmed to the corporation and body politic hereinbefore created; and that the said corporation and body politic may apply to its uses, and for the purpose of completing the erection of the monument aforesaid, according to such by-laws, rules, and regulations, as it may, from time to time, hereafter make and ordain, any and all property, of any and every kind and description whatsoever, which is now appertaining to said monument, or which the corporation and body politic hereby created may hereafter acquire, by purchase, gift, or other lawful means.

Sec. 3. *And be it further enacted,* That it shall be competent for the persons hereinbefore named and described as constituting the corporation and body politic hereby created, and their successors, to remove, by a vote of four-fifths of the said persons, any of their number; and the person so named shall no longer be a member of said corporation and body politic, nor have any authority therein: *Provided*, That for any other act within the legitimate objects of this corporation a quorum of five shall be sufficient for the transaction of business: *Provided*, That notice of all meetings which may not be provided for in the by-laws and ordinances of the corporation shall be given to all members thereof residing within the District of Columbia.

Sec. 4. *And be it further enacted*, That when any vacancy shall happen in the said corporation, and body politic, from death or resignation, or otherwise, the remaining members thereof shall elect and appoint a successor to fill the same, within ten days after the happening of such vacancy; and that on failure to file the same within thirty days, it shall be the duty of the attorney of the United States for the District of Columbia to proceed against the said corporation and body politic, by a writ of *scire facias*, for a forfeiture of the charter hereby granted, before the Circuit Court of the District of Columbia, and the adjudication of that court thereon shall be conclusive. And should this charter be so adjudged forfeited, the monument and other improvements and property held under the same shall be placed by the President of the United States under the care and custody of the Commissioner of Public Buildings, or such other officer of the United States as he may designate or appoint for the time being.

Sec. 5. *And be it further enacted*, That the said corporation and body politic, hereinbefore created, shall, by the name and style of the "Washington National Monument Society," have perpetual succession, shall be capable to sue or to be sued, to plead or be impleaded in any court of law or equity in the United States; may have and use a common seal, and the same may destroy, alter, and renew at pleasure, and shall have power to purchase, take, receive, and enjoy, to them and their successors, any and all property, of any kind and description whatsoever, for the purpose of completing the erection of said monument; to dispose of the same as they shall deem most conducive to the object of completing the erection now in progress of the monument aforesaid; to elect, so soon after the passage of this act as may be convenient, such officers as they may deem proper, and to make and ordain such constitution, by-laws, ordinances and regulations, consonant to the objects of this charter, as they may deem expedient and proper, and which shall not be repugnant to the Constitution and laws of the United States; and to repeal, alter, and amend the same: *Provided, always*, That the President of the United States for the time being shall be *ex officio* president, and the governors for the time being of the several States of the United States shall be respectively *ex officio* vice presidents of the said society, corporation, and body politic, and that all meetings thereof shall be held and all records and papers thereof kept at the said city of Washington.

Sec. 6. *And be it further enacted*, That this act may at any time be altered, amended, or repealed by the Congress of the United States.

Sec. 7. *And be it further enacted*, That all laws, acts, or resolutions, or any part of any law, act, or resolution, inconsistent with this act, shall be and the same are hereby repealed.

Sec. 8. *And be it further enacted*, That this act shall be in force from and after the passage thereof.

Sec. 9. *And be it further enacted*, That nothing in this act shall be so construed as to authorize this said corporation to issue any note, token, device, scrip, or other evidence of debt to be used as a currency.

Sec. 10. *And be it further enacted*, That each of the corporators in the said corporation shall be held liable, in his individual capacity, for all the debts and liabilities of said corporation, however contracted or incurred, to be recovered by suit, as other debts or liabilities, before any court of competent jurisdiction: *Provided, however*, That nothing herein contained shall be so construed as to render said corporators in said corporation individually liable for any debt or liability contracted in the name or behalf of the Washington National Monument Society at any time prior to the twentieth day of October, one thousand eight hundred and fifty-eight. [Passed February 22d, 1859.] Approved February 26, 1859.

UofM

www.ingramcontent.com/pod-product-compliance
Lightning Source LLC
LaVergne TN
LVHW020741120826
845150LV00010B/2290
* 9 7 8 1 4 1 8 1 9 4 6 6 6 *